God's Love
Is Not Bound by
Time

MARGARET STEWART

WESTBOW
PRESS®
A DIVISION OF THOMAS NELSON
& ZONDERVAN

WestBow Press books may be ordered through booksellers or by contacting:

WestBow Press
A Division of Thomas Nelson & Zondervan
1663 Liberty Drive
Bloomington, IN 47403
www.westbowpress.com
844-714-3454

All Scripture quotations, unless otherwise indicated, are taken from the Holy
Bible, New International Version®, NIV®. Copyright ©1973, 1978, 1984, 2011 by
Biblica, Inc.® Used by permission of Zondervan. All rights reserved worldwide.
www.zondervan.com The "NIV" and "New International Version" are trademarks
registered in the United States Patent and Trademark Office by Biblica, Inc.®

Scripture quotations marked (NLT) are taken from the Holy
Bible, New Living Translation, copyright ©1996, 2004, 2015 by
Tyndale House Foundation. Used by permission of Tyndale House
Publishers, Carol Stream, Illinois 60188. All rights reserved.

ISBN: 978-1-6642-4903-5 (sc)
ISBN: 978-1-6642-4904-2 (e)

Library of Congress Control Number: 2021922336

Print information available on the last page.

WestBow Press rev. date: 11/17/2021

This book is dedicated to all those who have experienced an unexpected trial and, while they were looking for answers, found a response they were not seeking.

It was the worst of times
It was the best of times

Acknowledgments

To my daughter, who graciously came along and took on the difficult job of transcribing my chicken-scratch to the computer. I will be forever grateful!

To special friends M, S, B and L, who faithfully stood by me in prayer and encouragement throughout this project. Thank you so much for your friendship!

And especially to our dear Lord who gave me my marching orders and then patiently supported me through all of my doubts. If there is anything praiseworthy, the praise belongs solely to Him.

To my son, who was skeptical at the beginning of this project. He joined in at the end, making necessary revisions and readying the manuscript for the content edit. I am forever grateful to you too!

Introduction

Dear Reader,

You will find many references to Bible verses in this book. They are taken from the New International Version of the Bible unless otherwise noted. Feel free to get out your own Bible and compare, then underline or highlight any verses that have special meaning to you.

> *For everything that was written in the past was written to teach us, so that through endurance and the encouragement of the scriptures we might have hope.—Romans 15:4*

Do you sometimes wonder "Who is God?" In Exodus 34:6–7, God declares this about Himself: " ...The Lord, the COMPASSIONATE, and GRACIOUS God. Slow to anger, abounding in LOVE and FAITHFULNESS, maintaining LOVE to thousands and FORGIVING wickedness, rebellion and sin." And in Numbers 23:19, the Lord speaks through Balaam: "God is not a man that He should lie, nor a son of man that He should change his mind. Does He speak and then not act? Does He promise and not fulfill?"

May God's word refresh your soul, draw you closer to Himself, and encourage you on your journey. Truly we serve an awesome God! This is my story that I pray will bring Him glory.

Chapter 1

Only I [God] can tell you what is going to happen even before it happens …—Isaiah 46:10 (NLT)

Do you like life-changing surprises? I do not! If you are going to surprise me with a bouquet of flowers, well, that would be delightful. But a life-changing surprise? No thank you!

My worst of times began in December of 1995. A snowstorm had made its way to our area a few days before, and some icy spots were still clinging to the pavement. As I was leaving my job, walking through the parking lot to my car, I fell and broke my wrist.

After molding a cast for my forearm, the doctor said, "You will be out of work for three months while this heals."

It was during this time that a dear friend and coworker called to ask how I was getting along with an out-of-commission appendage. We chatted for a while, and then came a moment I will never ever forget. She said, "I believe the Lord has set you aside to get ready for the battle."

Battle? What battle? I don't like arguments, quarrels, and fights, never mind a *battle*! I don't even like the *word* battle. The dictionary defines *battle* as a conflict, struggle or fight—sometimes between two people. Now, I knew my marriage wasn't perfect, but after thirty-three years together, we rarely if ever fought. We didn't always agree on a matter, but we didn't fight about it. I usually just got my way, and we moved on.

You see, I was used to getting my own way. When I was young, family and friends often felt sorry for me because my mother had died when I was five years old. So they always gave me what I wanted. This continued as I got older, and I eventually entered into marriage wanting my own way. Isaiah 53:6 says, "All we like sheep have gone astray, we have turned each one to his OWN WAY ..." Now my *own way* was leading me down a path toward a battle I definitely didn't want any part of. But God in His grace was getting me ready. It wasn't going to be a total surprise.

While waiting for my wrist to heal, I turned to God's Word, the Bible. I didn't know what this battle was going to be about, but I asked God to speak to me through His Word. It was January 1996 when Isaiah 43 became His love letter to me.

Some may say, "How can something that was said to the nation of Israel so many, many years ago speak to you today?" I turned to Hebrews 4:12, which says, "The Word of God is living and active ..." It isn't dead on a shelf; it speaks to me today. It is a living Word. This is what God said in Isaiah 43:1–5:

I created you,
I formed you,
I have redeemed you,
I have summoned you by name,
You are mine ...

When [it is not a matter of *if* but *when*] you pass through the waters, I will be with you and through the rivers they will not sweep over you.

When [it is not a matter of *if* but *when*] you walk through the fire, you will not be burned; nor will the flame set you ablaze.

I am the Lord your God,

I am your Savior;

You are precious in my sight,

I love you,

Do not be afraid,

I am with you.

Wow! I began to think, *What is it I will be going through?* The words *water, rivers, fire,* and *flame* stood out. Although we can use all of these things for good, it seemed to me in this context that they were going to try to harm me.

In our nation recently, we have seen the horrible destruction that takes place when extremely strong winds and waves come ashore to a coastal city, and flooding rainwaters cause a river to overflow. Lives are lost, and property is destroyed. The raging fires in California and elsewhere resulted in house after house burned to the ground, leaving many with only the clothes on their backs.

I searched my Bible again, and I found in John 10:10 that there is one who comes to kill, steal, and destroy, but Jesus says, "I have come that they might have life and have it to the full." So I realized this battle might not have only physical and emotional components, but would be, more importantly, a spiritual battle with one who has the power to steal, kill, and destroy. This was frightening to me! It would be a battle for one's soul.

As I look back, I see this was much more serious than just a hurtful *worst of times* situation. I'd like to say I was on my knees pleading with the Lord for my husband's soul, but that would not be the truth. I was selfish and mostly concerned about how I was going to survive this battle. I wanted my way—a Cinderella happily-ever-after ending. But I had a lot to learn.

Thankfully, I knew only God was going to have the answers, so I was drawn back to my Bible and Isaiah 43. God overwhelmed me with wonderful facts and promises, which I clung to like one hanging on to a life preserver while drowning.

I had grown up in the church, had wonderful Sunday School teachers, good Bible teaching from the pulpit—but it wasn't until I attended a Billy Graham Crusade at Madison Square Garden in New York City when I was seventeen that I was confronted with the fact that salvation is not just about head knowledge. Salvation is about a moment in time when you acknowledge your sin and your need for a Savior.

It was in the quiet of my bedroom that night that I put my faith in the Son of God, Jesus Christ. I invited Him to be my Savior, claiming the shed blood of Jesus as payment for my redemption. I did nothing to deserve this; it was the finished work of Jesus on the cross that made my salvation possible. Ephesians 2:8–9 says, "For it is by grace you have been saved through faith, and this is not from yourselves. It is the gift of God, not by works so that no one can boast." I praise God that this was the beginning of a loving, living relationship with a loving, living God.

When I look at Isaiah 43:1—"I have redeemed you"—I know that this is true. Because it is true, I can trust and have confidence that other facts in the chapter are true, such as:

- The Lord has created me, formed me, calls me by name.
- I belong to Him.
- I am precious in His sight.
- He loves me.
- He is my Lord and my God.

Whatever I go through, He will be with me. So armed with these promises and the knowledge of His love for me, I am ready to move forward.

Chapter 2

Even a child is known by his actions.—Proverbs 20:11

But first I must go backward. How did we get to this place—a place where a battle is going to occur? I'll start with my husband's story.

My husband was born in 1940 in Louisville, Kentucky. His dad's job had transferred his parents from New Jersey. It wasn't long before they were transferred again—to Cleveland, Ohio, where a sister joined the family. As his father moved up the corporate ladder, Minneapolis, Minnesota was their next destination. When the family arrived to join Dad (who had gone ahead to the new job), Mom received the shocking news that Dad wanted a divorce.

My husband was now eight years old. In those days, when a divorce was taking place, the judge allowed the children to choose which parent they wanted to live with. My husband chose his father. This turned out not to be a great decision, as his father quickly remarried, and he and his new wife drank their way through the next few years. A half-brother and half-sister were soon added to the family. My husband was left without much love, attention, or nurturing during those formative years.

At age twelve, my husband moved in with his mother (who had remarried), his sister, and his stepsister. He had friends from school he hung around with. Elvis was his favorite entertainer, and he would be happy to show you his version of the "twist". When he was seventeen, his mother divorced her second husband, and Mom and her two kids moved back to New Jersey to be near family.

The teenage years are tough enough without all of these disruptions, but despite a new place to live, a new school, and new friends, my husband graduated high school in the class of 1958.

After high school, my husband went to live with his father and his father's third wife in Philadelphia. (His dad's climb up the corporate ladder was no more due to his drinking.) My husband dreamed of joining the armed forces, but the routine physical exposed a defect in his heart. When he was nineteen, the doctors repaired his heart valve by sewing it. He went back to his mother and sister in New Jersey to recuperate. This was in 1959, and the doctors did the best they could with the knowledge they had at that time. Their mending job lasted until 1982.

The year 1940 was also the year of my birth. I was born and raised in New Jersey and have lived there my whole life. My parents, along with my aunt and uncle, moved here from Pennsylvania in the 1930s, escaping a career in the coal mines. They opted to work instead for the Jersey Central Railroad.

When I was three years old, we moved from an apartment to a house. It was a nice house, but it was not a happy home. My father became a heavy drinker. At age five, I lost my mother to suicide. As to the *why*, I can only speculate, but I believe it was a combination of circumstances that were beyond her control, and perhaps she saw it as her only way out.

The memory of my mother faded rather quickly. I don't remember her at all—I only have pictures to look at. I don't remember anything of our relationship. It wasn't until I went through this difficult time in my life that I wished so much I could talk to her, cry with her, and be held in her arms.

My grandparents sold their home in Pennsylvania, bought our house from my father, and moved in to take care of me. But a year later, my father remarried and took me to live with him and his new wife. For me, the next two years were not the best of times. I was the other woman's child.

We moved three times in two years. I was now attending a religious school and a new church foreign to anything I had been exposed to before. And of course, every move meant finding new friends. During these two years, a half-brother and a half-sister were born. There was one period of time when my stepmother, father, brother, and I all slept in one room. I had a cot that was placed up against the door that went out to the hallway of the apartment building. In the winter, whenever anyone went in or out of the building, a cold blast of air found its way through the cracks in the door to me. There was also no heat in the bathroom—only icicles hanging. I don't think I took too many baths in those days.

My stepmother died in August 1948, giving birth to my half-sister. She had been in the hospital for two months prior to the birth with heart problems. When she went into the hospital, I was sent back to my grandparents to live—and I stayed there happily for the next six years. My half-brother and half-sister were sent to live with two separate sisters of their mother. I only saw them once or twice more in my lifetime.

My grandmother was my favorite person in the world. I loved her so much, and I knew with certainty that she loved me too. There was nothing she wouldn't do for me. Sewing was her expertise. She made all of my clothes and even made clothes for my dolls. In those days, we wore dresses to school (jeans were after-school garments).

My grandfather was very quiet. He worked in his garden in the summer and was an avid reader. It was my grandma and I who conversed and laughed together at the dinner table. I was privileged to take in all of her love and care for me, particularly the six years I was blessed to live with her and on until her passing in 1972.

Once I went to live with my grandparents, I never lived with my father again. Occasionally, he came to visit and have dinner with us, but these times grew further and further apart. One day when I was twelve years old, my father came to see me. He had a woman in the car, and he wanted me to go for a ride with them. I went to the car and met her and immediately knew I wanted no part of this relationship. I'd already had two mothers—that was enough!

We sat on the front porch, and I told him I didn't want to go with them. He said if I didn't go for a ride with them, I would never see him again. And so, I only saw my father briefly two more times until he died of cirrhosis of the liver when I was twenty-one years old.

Now I was a teenager—doing things teenagers do—and the adults in the family agreed that I needed some younger supervision, so I moved into my aunt and uncle's home a few blocks away. There I was well loved and cared for until I married at age twenty-four. As a family, we enjoyed playing a card game called Phooey whenever we could round up four players. Even one of our young neighbors used to come over to get in the game; however, if he lost, he would tear up the scoresheet!

My uncle always had a joke to tell that made you laugh, and a candy kiss to pass out to all of the kids after Sunday church service. My aunt was a nurse, compassionate and caring, keeping the family balanced and in order. Their two sons, my cousins, made the family complete.

One of the most influential things in my life from third grade through part of high school was Girl Scouts. We had a wonderful, well-organized leader. I learned skills I still use today and earned many badges. We went camping together and even took a weeklong trip to Girl Scout headquarters, where we slept in tents and visited many historic places in Washington, DC. I made lifelong friendships, and it is an experience I am very grateful to have had.

After high school, I went to work at Bell Laboratories. I began in the mailroom, worked in the filing department for four years, and then (along with another gal) held the position of receptionist for all five thousand employees, greeting people from around the world. My career at Bell Labs lasted for ten years.

That's a brief look at our childhood, with marriage on the horizon. Were we ready?

Chapter 3

Therefore what God has joined together, let man not separate.—Matthew 19:6

It wasn't until 1963 that my husband and I met. Attending a church group for single young adults, we noticed that we were wearing high school rings from the same school. Upon closer examination, we discovered that we had been in the same graduating class (along with approximately four hundred other students), so the conversations began. Dating followed.

We always felt comfortable with each other, and those long evening chats revealed we had much in common. We both claimed Jesus as our Lord and Savior; we attended different churches, but the same denomination; and our ethnic backgrounds were similar. We had both experienced a few bumps in our childhoods; neither of us had gone further than high school in our education; and we just enjoyed being together. It wasn't long before we declared our love for one another.

I was a patient of the dentist my husband's mother worked for, and she encouraged him to date me. My grandfather had a good friend in the "old guard" group who was also my husband's grandfather's best friend. So there was a thumbs-up from family members to continue this relationship.

Well, all except for my aunt. Being a nurse, she was concerned about his heart in light of his recent operation. She was also worried about his model of marriage, with his parents both being married three times and divorced twice. She expressed her concerns to me, and I replied, "But … but … but … he's a nice guy …" He took me on fun dates. He was a gentleman—opening the car door for me, seating me at the table, etc. He gave a lot of thought to how he showed his love for me. For example, on our one-month anniversary of dating (paper), he sent me a telegram declaring his love for me. Second month (cotton), he bought me two cotton blouses. Third month, a beautiful diamond ring complete with staging—record player playing my song while, on his knees, he asked, "Will you marry me?" We were married exactly one year from our first date.

Between several bridal showers and the generous wedding gifts from family and friends, settling into married life came easily. We were married May 2, 1964. To make the ceremony more meaningful, we memorized our vows. My dress and flowers were everything I had ever dreamed of, and of course, it was a day I will never forget.

We set up housekeeping in a second-floor apartment in a neighboring town. We both worked. Our families lived nearby, and we could do whatever we wanted when we wanted to. We were very happy, and I remember us lying in bed and vowing to each other that we would never get divorced.

One good decision we made in the early years of our marriage was to never drink liquor again. With a history of each of our fathers being an alcoholic, we made this vow and immediately threw whatever liquor we had in the house down the drain. It was a dramatic scene and not a decision for everyone, but it was the right one for us.

Chapter 4

Children are a gift from the Lord, they are a reward from Him.—Psalm 127:3 (NTL)

I continued to work for three more years after we were married, and by then starting a family was the plan. Three more years, and still no little one. I wasn't getting my way, so I put into motion a plan to fix that. I suggested adoption to my husband, and he agreed.

Although I may have had a selfish motive, I know now that this was all part of God's plan. We started interviews with a local agency, and nine months later, an adorable two-month-old baby girl in a pretty pink dress found her way to our address. She was the most perfect baby. She was, and continues to be, the perfect complement to our family, and she has expressed many times how thankful she is to be a part of our family.

After thirteen years of marriage, I gave birth to a son. To say that we were thrilled would be an understatement! Two and a half years later, I gave birth to our second son. I was forty years old now, and our nest was full. We had a daughter entering her teenage years, a toddler, and a baby. Life was busy, with cleaning, laundry, grocery shopping, ironing, reading to the little ones, potty training, fixing meals—all the usual things that take up a mom's time. Don't get me wrong: I was happy in this role. I had played house with my dolls when I was young, and now I was living the real thing.

But it all took time. Was I taking time away from my husband? I didn't see it that way, but perhaps he did. The first red flag was about to go up.

One of my girlfriends attended a church meeting

where my husband was present. My nice guy offered to give her a ride home. The next day, she was on the phone telling me that I needed to pay more attention to my husband. It was true that I used to get annoyed with him when he called from work on his lunch hour just to say hi. I was usually in the middle of something, and he had nothing important to say. But she was right: I should be grateful he was calling me and not some other woman. There were more of these red-flag days in the coming years, but for various reasons, I never took them as a real threat. But we were growing apart, and intimacy was becoming a thing of the past.

The 1980s had some memorable moments. My husband had his second open-heart operation; this time, the doctors inserted a titanium valve in his heart that would be effective for the rest of his life. We lost four loving family members who had been very influential in our lives: my husband's grandfather, his father, and my aunt and uncle. Our daughter graduated high school, bound for college. And I returned to the workforce.

Both my husband and I wanted our children to attend Christian school. This was important to us, and we were willing to sacrifice to make this possible. But by the time our daughter was a sophomore in high school, the grass was looking a little greener on the other side. Our third child was entering kindergarten, and the budget was being stretched thin. Our daughter was begging to go to the public school, so we gave our OK.

My husband consulted an experienced Christian gentleman concerning our budget. The advice he received was that we could no longer afford the Christian school, and we should sell our house and move to another neighborhood. Well, this was *not* what I wanted to hear. I had to fix this—so I got a job.

This is not advice for other people—each one has a different situation—but I think we all try to do what we think is right at the time. In my case, looking back, I don't think this actually was the right decision. My husband worked either the nine-to-five or the three-to-eleven shift. When he worked three to eleven, he had too much time on his hands before work each day, and no purposeful way to fill it.

Chapter 5

Sin is crouching at your door, it desires to have you, but you must master it.—Genesis 4:7

Eighteen months after I was warned of an impending battle, I found the battlefield had been chosen, and the players were about to be identified.

Our youngest son was a junior in high school. While I was at work on June 12, 1997, I received a phone call from our son's school saying that he had plans to commit suicide and I needed to come to school immediately. Thankfully, his plans were thwarted when the student he confided this to reported it. I picked him up from school, and we drove to the doctor's office. After examining him, the doctor prescribed medication. In the adjoining office, there was a psychologist, and an appointment was quickly arranged. After *much, much* coaxing, my son started with counseling (and continued for several years).

The next day, June 13, 1997, after dinner, I suddenly found myself going outside to my husband's car. When inside, I opened the glove compartment. I have no idea what made me do this—I had never done it before and have never done it since. I found many cash-advance slips that he was hiding and items I didn't even know what they were for.

My husband came running out the door to ask me what I was doing. When I showed him what I had found, the lies began. After some nasty words between us, my husband said he would tell me the whole story on his birthday, August 5—fifty-three days away.

I was angry. I was sad. I was tired. I didn't know what

to do next for our son. With all of this on my mind, I agreed to his ridiculous plan of waiting.

Within twenty-four hours, I had discovered that my son was suicidal and my husband was unfaithful. I was overwhelmed with sadness. How did this happen? Oh, how I needed those promises from the Lord! I felt like my heart was going to break. This way was *not* my way. I wanted to close my eyes, wake up, and find that it was all a bad dream.

Do you think the Lord had my attention?

It was summertime now. School was out (I also worked at a school), and there was time to think about what had happened and what could be done about it. As I usually found myself in control of situations, I had to learn this was one time I could not fix the problem. I had to let go and let God take control. Not easy to do when you've been having your way for fifty-seven years. It was like the Lord was saying, "You can't heal your son, and you can't change your husband. You have lost control. It is no longer *your way*. I have allowed these drastic things to happen for a purpose, but keep trusting me, and we will get through this together."

I turned in my Bible to Psalm 23:4, which spoke to me about "walking through the valley." The word *through* caught my eye like never before. We are not dying in the valley; we are not even lingering there. We are passing through.

These may be shadowy, dark, and difficult days, but I was only on a journey to higher ground with my Lord. Take Him at His word: "Lo I am with you always." Through the heart-wrenching times, God is there. The lessons He is going to teach me could not be learned from a book, only through experience.

In July of that year, there was a period of three days when the mailman passed by our house. We always got mail, even if it was just junk mail. I confronted the mailman, and he said, "Oh, your husband put a stop on the mail—your mail is at the post office."

Immediately, I drove to the post office, and upon opening the mail, I found a credit card bill with a charge I couldn't account for. I questioned my husband when he got home from work. At first, he said he couldn't remember what it was for, but later he admitted he had charged a birthday gift for a girl he was calling his "soul mate." Ouch, that hurt!

If you asked me for words to describe my marriage at this point, I would say: deceit, sneaky, lies, betrayal, cheating, secrets, uncommitted. A marriage has to be built on trust. In this marriage, trust had packed up and left.

Our song was a beautiful, romantic song entitled "More Today Than Yesterday". A portion of the lyrics are "I love you more today than yesterday but not as much as tomorrow." What happened to the times when we used to say those words to each other and then argue over who loved the other more? Where did those days go?

Chapter 6

The lips of an adulteress drip honey, her speech is smoother than oil. Keep to a path far from her. Do not go near the door to her house.—Proverbs 5:3 and 5:8

The calendar said August 5. It was time to talk. I was pretty much aware by now of what my husband had been up to, but how did this happen?

He told his story: One day, he decided to go for a massage, and finding it felt so good, he made plans to go again. He went from parlor to parlor until one day he found one that did more than massages.

I asked him, "What do you think the Lord thinks about your behavior?"

He answered, "That's between me and the Lord."

Very often, these girls are from another country. I knew he had purchased a Bible written in Russian for one of them. He said he was telling these girls about the Lord. I guess he thought he was their personal evangelist. My Bible called it adultery, and one of the Ten Commandments is "Do not commit adultery." Does God give a command and then give you a wink when you disobey, just because you are talking about Him? I don't think God is in the winking business. He means what he says.

When God says *do not* in the Bible, He is not doing this to be mean. He says *do not* out of His love for us, because He knows what the consequences will be if we *do*. God is providing a boundary for our protection, a pathway to safety and freedom.

The Bible speaks about marriage. In the New Living Translation, Paul records some suggestions on the subject, such as 1 Corinthians 6:18, 7:3: "Run away from sexual sin! No other sin so clearly affects the body as this one does. The husband should not deprive his wife of sexual intimacy that is her right as a married woman, nor should the wife deprive her husband." I know it takes two to tango, so I take a portion of the blame. That I had to confess.

My husband said he was sorry, and it was now my responsibility to forgive him. Forgiving people doesn't necessarily mean that what they did is OK with you or that they deserve to be forgiven. In Ephesians 4:32, the Lord says I am to forgive others because even when I didn't deserve it, He forgave me. It is an act of my will and releases me from becoming bitter about the situation.

I asked my husband to tell the children, ages seventeen, twenty, and twenty-seven, what was going on because I didn't want them to hear it from the grapevine. I was also up-front with them in explaining that I had lost interest in intimacy. I guess I shouldn't have been too concerned about the grapevine, because who was I going to discuss this with? As a child, you run to Mommy to tell her your troubles, but I felt like I had no one. Family members had passed away, and I wasn't ready to speak about this intimate problem with even my closest friends. It is not exactly something you want shouted from the pulpit on Sunday morning.

I was frantically looking for a book that would give me a 1-2-3 lesson of what to do so that life would be back to "happily ever after," but none was found. There are many books on marriage, but I never found one that spoke to my particular situation.

Matthew 11:28 reads, "The Lord says come to me all you who are weary and burdened and I will give you rest." I was burdened, and my heart was very heavy. God's words of encouragement were such a blessing during this time, but one day I found that there was something I needed. I woke up on Sunday morning and said to the Lord, "I really need a hug."

We went to church, and after the service, a group of people gathered in the vestibule, chatting with each other. A gentleman who used to belong to our church but was now a missionary was visiting that morning, and he came up to me and gave me a big hug. Of course, he had no idea what I had said to the Lord earlier, but I know that hug was straight from the Lord. He even cares about the small details of our lives. Amazing!

We went the usual route of counseling and a support group for my husband. My greatest help came from the Lord. Psalm 46:1 says, "God is our refuge and strength. An ever-present help in trouble." And although I would like to hurry up and fix this trouble, the Lord said to me, "Be still and know that I am God" (Psalm 46:10).

There was a battle going on for my husband's soul. He was on a slippery slope downward. His whole personality was changing: he had trouble sleeping, couldn't concentrate, lost his appetite, was angry and irritable, became overly concerned with his appearance, was critical, needed more money for himself, and said he didn't love me anymore. Ouch! That hurt!

> *A double minded man is unstable in*
> *all his ways.—James 1:8 (KJV)*

> *For though we live in the world, we do not*
> *wage war as the world does.—2 Corinthians*
> *10:3*

Jesus is our example in Luke 4:1–13. When Jesus was in the desert for forty days and had nothing to eat, the devil came to him and tempted him three times. Each time, Jesus answered the devil with scripture. One of our weapons in spiritual warfare is God's Word. Ephesians 6:17 tells us that among our arsenal of weapons is the sword of the Spirit, which is the Word of God.

During the summer, the Lord led me to words of encouragement in the Bible, such as Psalm 27:13: "I am still confident of this; I will see the goodness of the Lord in the land of the living." I felt for sure that while I was still alive, I would see goodness come out of this situation. Isaiah 64:4 says, "God … acts on behalf of those who wait for Him." When I stopped to consider this, I was awestruck to think that God, the Creator of the universe, was working on my behalf. But there is a condition attached to this promise. I must wait. Wait for Him to work out His purpose, in His timing.

Waiting is never fun. Waiting in the dentist office, in line at the grocery store, for the results from a test, or waiting on the Lord. If we exercise our patience, we will be able to witness the Lord in action. If we don't wait and run ahead of Him, we will miss the peace we can have knowing He is in control instead of us. We will miss experiencing the wonder of His power and the realization of the extent He is willing to go, all because He loves us.

I had to remember that in God's economy, nothing is wasted: not our waiting, not our questions, not even our broken hearts. He uses everything to teach us and draw us closer to Himself if we allow Him. Every circumstance in our life, God can use to ultimately bring glory to Him.

While I was waiting, I tried to have fun each day looking for things I was thankful for, big or small. I made a list. Here is a sampling:

1. I was thankful my grandparents gave me an appreciation for fine music. We didn't have a TV when I was young, so we gathered around the radio on Monday nights, when beautiful music was scheduled. My grandmother also listened to live operas from the Metropolitan Opera on Saturday afternoons.

2. I was thankful for my teeth. I had just been to the dentist and received a good report.
3. I was thankful for good friends.
4. I was thankful for the beautiful colored leaves.

I made it a game. The Lord said in 1 Thessalonians 5:18, "Give thanks in ALL circumstances for this is God's will for you in Christ Jesus." Giving thanks, no matter how small, changes our outlook and our attitude.

Chapter 7

Why are you downcast, oh my soul? ... Put your hope in God!—Psalm 42:5

We all want to support our children, whether it's a music recital, a sports game, or the dark days of depression. The summer was over, but our son was not himself. Senior year was on the schedule for school, but after a few days of class, he found it too hard to get out of bed. He withdrew more and more into himself, and he wouldn't (or couldn't) talk to me. It was the most awful feeling: the child who had always brought me so much joy was now not speaking to me.

I began to think how sad the Lord must feel when we don't take time to talk to Him. There is nothing I wouldn't do for my son; what could I do to unleash him from this dark place he was in? Again, I thought of the Lord. He proved there was nothing He wouldn't do for us when He sent his son Jesus to die on the cross for our sins.

I had come to a point where I recognized my child was only on loan from the Lord. God was the one who had created him, knit him together in the womb, and knew all about him (Psalm 139:13). When something needs help, like a shoe that needs repair, where do you go? To the shoemaker. So, when our bodies need help, where should we go? To the one who created them.

It was recorded in the books of Matthew, Mark, Luke, and John in the Bible that Jesus did many marvelous things for people. He healed the blind so they could see, the lame so they could walk, the deaf so they could hear, and those with evil spirits he made well. We are aware of what Jesus is able to do—that nothing is impossible with Him. I must let go and release my son to the Lord and pray for God's will.

Our son agreed he needed help. We chose a hospital and drove him there with the anticipation he would receive help with medication, counseling, and support groups. As it turned out, the experience was not all we had hoped for, so we brought him home.

The good that came out of his hospital stay was that he decided from then on to take his medication. Up until this time, he confessed he was only pretending to take his pills. He called them his "happy pills," and he didn't want to feel happy because the pill was making him happy. He wanted to feel happy because he was truly happy.

At this time, our son returned to school.

The holidays came and went, and it was a new year—1998. Because our son was still struggling, he proposed a plan. He wanted to leave school with the promise of returning in the fall and repeating the first half of his senior year. When he was having trouble concentrating, it was hard to achieve the good grades he was used to. My husband and I had our doubts about this plan and the staff at school was very skeptical, pointing out that most children who drop out of school do not return. We, along with the staff at school, had a lot to learn about our son's character.

Our son left school and began working at a gas station. The beginning of April, he tried again to commit suicide, and once more the Lord intervened. The Lord has a plan and a purpose for him, and this was not it. Now our son was seeing a psychiatrist, and the prescribed medication was helping.

Our son continued working at the gas station. It was good for him. It gave him some pocket money and the opportunity to interact with customers; kept him busy; and gave him a reason to get up in the morning.

I am very proud to say our son returned to school in September 1998. That was not an easy step for him to take, because all the students he had been with since kindergarten had now graduated.

In Psalm 66:12 of my Bible, there is a date written in the margins: *October 6, 1998*. It was on this date that the Lord said to me, "… we went through fire and water …" It was in the *past tense*. The battle was going to be over. I didn't know when, but it was going to come to an end.

It was a very special moment when we watched our son walk across the stage to receive his diploma in June 1999. With all he had been through, we were so very proud of him. He continued his education, graduating from a local community college and then making the comment "enough school." He has been working ever since.

In 2007, our son attempted suicide again, and once again, the Lord spared his life. In 2013, he made the decision to go off all medication. He is glad not to be dependent on the medicine anymore. Some days are better than others; his battle isn't over yet.

Once again, I turn to the fact that my timing is not the Lord's timing. The example of Lazarus in John 11:1–44 reminds me of that. Lazarus was sick, and his sister sent word to Jesus, "Lord, the one you love is sick," hoping that Jesus would come quickly and heal him. But instead, Jesus waited two more days. Verse 14 tells us He did this on purpose so that people would believe in Him. And if they believed, they would witness the glory of God. Lazarus died, and Jesus came and raised him from the dead, an even greater accomplishment than if he had hurried to them and healed him.

God's delay in answering is not a sign of His indifference to our situation. While He is never late, His timing rarely coincides with ours. Waiting a few days may have made Jesus late for a healing, but it made Him right on time for a resurrection. Trusting His schedule is not always easy, but it is something I must learn.

Jesus said in verses 25 and 26, "I am the resurrection

and the life. He who believes in me will live, even though he dies, and whoever lives and believes in me will never die. Do you believe this?" And the same question comes to us today. Do you believe in Jesus the Son of God? Have you ever asked Jesus to be your Savior? If not and you would like to, here is a simple prayer you can pray:

> *Dear God, search my heart. I confess my sins before you. I believe Jesus is the son of God, that he died for my sins, and that He has risen from the dead. I invite Jesus into my heart and life to help me to live a life pleasing to You. In Jesus's name, Amen.*

John 3:16 says, "For God so loved the world that He gave His one and only son that whoever believes in Him shall not perish but have eternal life." Having eternal life is not something you have to guess about. Do you or don't you have eternal life? God has made it clear in John 5:13: "I (John) write these things to you who believe in the name of the Son of God so that you may know that you have eternal life."

I am trusting my son into the Lord's care and have faith that his story will one day bring glory to God.

Chapter 8

So then, each of us will give an account of himself to God.—Romans 14:12

My husband was a faithful employee for twenty-eight years. In 1993, he was offered a package of benefits to leave his job. The company called it *downsizing*. I saw it as a way for the corporation to save money on his pension, because at thirty years' service, the pension would have increased. My husband took the package, retired, and was immediately hired by an outside contractor to work at the same company doing the same job. After five more years, that ended, and he was filing for unemployment.

During this time, the Lord's provisions came in many unexpected ways. There was a honey-baked ham for our Christmas dinner from our oldest son's job; a beautiful Christmas tree was purchased for us; a neighbor brought over loaves of bread every week until my husband had steady work; and we received coupons to be used at a local grocery store, just to mention a few. God is so good, and we were very thankful.

My husband tried selling cars at a local dealership (he always loved cars), but financially, it didn't work out. Eventually, he took a job as a security guard, where he worked until he officially retired in 2007. I asked him to sell his car (which was his favorite car he ever owned) to pay off some of the debts he had accrued, and he did. His behavior came to a stop with no car and no money.

For the next four years, until his death, we did things together like grocery shopping, watching TV, and eating our meals, but things were never the same. My husband had become a prisoner in his mind. He admitted that he thought about this girl all the time and pined for her. I, on the other hand had become a prisoner in my body. Over the years, I had gained a lot of weight. I enjoyed eating— particularly sweets, and yes, the Lord has something to say about that too. Proverbs 23:2 says, "Put a knife to your throat if you are given to gluttony." I don't think the Lord wants us to die, but he is making a strong point that excessive indulgence in food is not good.

The Lord didn't make us robots. He gave us minds to choose His way or our way. We can put the blame on our genes or whatever else we want to come up with, but the truth is, we are each responsible for the decisions we make. Sin is sin, whether it's a sexual sin or an overeating sin. It's going our own way, doing what we want. 1 John 1:9 says, "If we confess our sins, He (God) is faithful and just and will forgive our sins and purify us from all unrighteousness." Forgiveness is not a right; we don't deserve it, but God in his mercy is willing to forgive us when we confess to Him what we have done and turn away from it. We can be forgiven, but most often we are left with the consequences of our sin.

A drastic example of consequences paid for sin is found in the book of Numbers in my Bible: chapters 13 and 14. Moses had asked twelve men, one from each tribe, to go and scout out the land God had promised the Israelites. After forty days of exploration, they returned. Ten of the men reported the land was good for farming, but the people were like giants, and the cities were fortified and very large. Only two, Joshua and Caleb, were willing to take God at His word and move forward to possess the land.

The bad reports spread among the people, and they grumbled against their leader Moses. Moses interceded and asked God to forgive the people for their unbelief (verse 19). God forgave them (verse 20), but there was a severe consequence. They had to wander in the desert for forty years. That was one year for each day the men had explored the land.

During those years, every person who was presently twenty years of age or older would die. Not one of them, except for Joshua and Caleb, would enter the promised land. Because of their trusting God and their obedience and wanting to go forward with God's plan, they were the only two of that generation to enter the promised land. Obedience is so important if we don't want to suffer unwelcome consequences from going our own way.

It needs to be noted here that although God had to discipline the Israelites during this time, out of His love He provided food (manna) for the people for forty years. Their clothes never wore out, and their feet never got swollen (Deuteronomy 8:3–4). God still loved them, and He showed it in a tangible way while He was disciplining them. And isn't that just how we should discipline our children? Set consequences for wrongdoing, but making it known that we still love them.

Our wedding vows "for better or worse, richer or poorer, in sickness and in health—until death do us part" had been made before God, and they were still in my mind. Because we had memorized them, I will never forget them. We had been there for each other through the financial struggles, through sickness and health, through the better times and now the worst of times. God had been there through it all also.

We had been married almost forty-seven years when my husband died in 2011. Before he died, he said to me, "I can't die. You need me." It was true, I needed him, but knowing in the end he was concerned for me and maybe still loved me was all I really needed. Isn't this sometimes like our relationship with God? By nature, I seem to always want to know the details: the who, what, when, and why of the situation. But God in his soft voice whispers, "You are loved, and that's all you really need to know."

Little did my husband realize that our children would step up to the plate and take good care of their mom. His battle is over. Now it is really between him and the Lord.

All three of our children have been married. There have been a few divorces, but I am blessed to have three precious grandchildren who bring me much joy. Proverbs 17:6 says, "Children's children are a crown to the aged."

Chapter 9

We live by faith, not by sight.—2 Corinthians 5:7

My life experiences are coming to a close, but first I must return to chapter 7 of this book and the verse Psalm 66:12: "We went through fire and water …" The first time I read this verse in 1998, I immediately drew a conclusion that because the word *went* was past tense, the battle must be going to end soon. I admitted I didn't know when, but I assumed the battle was not going to last long.

But it doesn't say that! You see, the Lord is still teaching me. Although we went through many skirmishes, the promise has not been totally fulfilled yet. Our *went* is still in progress. We still have life experiences to go through.

God brought me to Hebrews chapter 11, one of my favorites on the subject of faith. Verse 1 explains what faith is: "Now faith is being sure of what we hope for and certain of what we do not see." A list of many people of faith from the Old Testament follows. These people were still living by faith when they died.

In Genesis 17:8, God gave Abraham a promise: "The whole land of Canaan [now Israel] I will give as an everlasting possession to you and your descendants after you …" God renewed this promise to Abraham's son Isaac in Genesis 26:2–4: "For to you and your descendants I will give all these lands and will confirm the oath I swore to your father Abraham." And to Isaac's son Jacob, God said, "I will give you and your descendants the land on which you are lying" (Genesis 28:13).

Jacob's son Joseph received the same promise in Genesis 50:24: "God will take you out of this land to the land he promised on oath to Abraham, Isaac and Jacob." None lived to see the promise fulfilled, and yet they had faith that one day this was going to happen. So much so that as Joseph was dying, he made his brothers promise that they would carry his bones with them when they entered the promised land (verse 25).

The descendants of Abraham were slaves in Egypt for 430 years (Exodus 12:40). Exodus 13:19 tells us that Moses took the bones of Joseph with him when he and the Israelites fled Egypt because he knew of the promise that had been made hundreds of years before. It took them another forty years after they fled Egypt to receive what God had promised. Joshua chapter 3 tells that story.

Now I must ask myself: do I have a faith like Abraham, Isaac, Jacob, and Joseph? Do I have a faith as small as a mustard seed (Matthew 17:20)? Does my faith acknowledge that nothing will be impossible with God (Luke 1:37)? Is it a faith that is not dependent on some formula but rather a faith that still trusts God to keep His promise to me that the battle will be a *went* of the past someday?

"Jesus Christ is the same yesterday, today and forever" (Hebrews 13:8). What He has done in the past, He can do now and in the future. He is *able*! In the meantime, I have faith He will fulfill His promise in His time and His way.

Be sure of what we hope for and certain of what we do not see …

This is faith!

Chapter 10

As for God, His Way is perfect.—2 Samuel 22:31
Jesus said, "Follow Me."—Mark 2:14

Never in a million years would I have thought that when I was fifty-seven years old, I would be going through the worst of times in my life. It certainly wasn't my time or my way. The Lord allowed these circumstances to get my attention to humble me and to teach me. Even at eighty years old, I am still learning!

I have been a widow now for ten years. I miss my husband, the "nice guy." My mind has happy memories, but it also has many, many regrets. I'd love to live my life over with what I know now, but that won't happen. I am most thankful for my Lord and Savior Jesus Christ, who saw me through the worst of times but who also brought me to the best of times as He led me step by step through His Word. It was His Word that brought me comfort, His Word that encouraged me along the way, and His Word that disciplined me.

He taught me that it is not about things going MY WAY; it's about following Him and going HIS WAY. Proverbs 16:9 says, "A man's heart plans his way, but the Lord directs his steps." Praise God, He loves us so much He doesn't leave us where we are, but He prunes us and then prunes us some more so we can bloom and bear fruit for Him.

As a Christian, one of my goals is to be a blessing to others. 2 Corinthians 1:3–4 says that it is the man (or woman) who has gone through the dark valleys who can comfort and encourage others in similar situations. That is one of my purposes in writing this book. I pray that reading about my life experiences has been an encouragement to you—not because of me but because of who Jesus is (the Son of God) and what He's able to do.

Know that God loves you no matter what circumstances you are in. He doesn't want you to stop or linger in that valley. Keep going to higher ground where you can find a renewed love for the Lord Jesus and a deeper trust, confidence, and faith in the lover of your soul. To God be the glory!

Printed in the United States
by Baker & Taylor Publisher Services